The Rhythm of Time

Insightful Words of Hope & Encouragement

Poetry

by Karen Klassen

The Rhythm of Time

The Scribe's Closet Publications
702 South Missouri Street
Macon, MO 63552

www.thescribesclosetpublications.com

First Printing 2015

ISBN 978-1-943058-00-6

Helen Neustaedter
February 5, 1924 ~ September 29, 2014

This book is dedicated to my mom,
who was always there for me,
encouraging me, praying for me and
reminding me that I can make it,
even through the most difficult times of my life.

Although for years we lived many miles apart,
we always enjoyed a closeness
that geography could not influence.
She was by far not perfect,
but she was my mother
and I honored her and loved her.

Acknowledgement

I want to acknowledge all those who believe I have a gift for writing poetry, and have kept nudging me all these years to publish and share my work.

I thank my husband for his encouragement and honesty when reading my poems.

I also want to especially mention and thank my friend, Patsy Lemke, who did the proof reading and made the necessary changes to have my thoughts worded correctly.

I thank my publisher, who helped gather these moments of inspiration for this book and made it look more like the image I had in mind.

And lastly, I want to acknowledge all who have been an inspiration for me to either write a poem about you or about something you were going through. Thank you for being part of my life and thus making it fuller and richer!

I thank God for the many times He's awakened me to go to my desk and start writing. I acknowledge Him as my director and guide. He has given me a gift to encourage others through poetry.

To Him be all the glory.

Dear Reader:

I have often wondered why a person would be so compelled to write a poem.

When the nudging to start writing would come, I couldn't seem to ignore it. It wouldn't leave me alone until I would get to my computer and begin typing the words that seemed to be swirling around in my head.

I didn't particularly think of myself as artistic or talented, and it never really crossed my mind that someday I would have enough poems to publish a book. In the past I've often been encouraged to write about my adventures and experiences as a missionary. But a book of poems... Really?

Yet here it is...a collection of different moments in life that spurred the birth of yet another poem.

My hope and prayer is that whenever you pick up this book, you will find the right poem to give you just what you need for that moment, whether it's hope, faith, love, direction, encouragement or just a reminder that you can make it and are not alone in this circumstance of life.

May just the right page open for you!

~ Karen Klassen

Table of Contents

Poems about Difficult Times in Life

Poems of Faith and Commitment

Poems about Life and Death

Poems about
Special People in Life

Poems of Hope and Forgiveness

Time

Time is precious
Once lost it cannot be regained
If wasted it is hard to explain
If given
will make a life richer

Time can make a friend
Mend a heart
It can seem forever
or give you a new start

Time is a gift
Given from above
Lord help me today
with the time I've been given

The Perfect Plan

Long ago it all started
The forming of God's perfect plan
The day the universe was created
And hung in space made by His hand

He made time and brought it to existence
To be used a powerful tool
It brings order yet has a limit
If abused makes one a fool

He filled the earth with life and colors
Bringing brightness to each day
And for night time hung the moon
And the stars to direct our way

Stepping back He observed creation
No equal beauty could one find
Yet yearning fellowship and communion
God longed for one of his own kind

Creating man in His own image
He gave him rule over all creation
And the choice to give back to his maker
His life, all praise and adoration

Yet over time man left his maker
Striving to do things his own way
Pain and hardship where now his companions
As he sinned and went astray

God's plan then came to fruition
He sent His Son for sin to pay
Death was the price for our atonement
Christ conquered death and rose from the grave

He gave us hope for life eternal
His Spirit to guide and direct our way
His mercy and peace to live life in victory
And all we have to do is accept Him today

Psalm 91

14

Poems of Comfort
and
Encouragement

Angels

God you give your angels the command
To watch over us and keep us from harm
And when we grow weary and can't walk anymore
You send your angels to pick us up and carry us on

Lord when strongholds rise up against us
Your angels are there to fight for us in battle
Setting a standard against the enemy
They help us rise up to sing a victory song

God you commission your angels
To overshadow us with your mercy and grace
They surround us with your love and show us clearly
That only under your wings can we truly be safe

Remember

Remember.....
God promised he'd never give us
More than we can bear
Though there are times when we want
To shout "Lord this isn't fair"
God reaches down in his love
And says "Child give me your hand
I'll walk here beside you and
Carry that load
Just lean on me and lift up your eyes
For over that hill your victory lies"

Peace & Rest

There are times when Peace is hard to find
When troubles seem to crowd our mind
When our heart feels heavy with a load of sin and
There seems little way for God's light to shine in

There are times when rest is what we seek
Striving to find it we become weak
We search with a need from within to hear
Our Father's assurance that He is still near

Yet through these times we continue to grow
With a deepening understanding we also know
That the peace and rest we strive to receive
Are all part of Christ in us who believe

The word of God seems to penetrate
As in worship we read and praises make
Then our spirit soars and we rise above
And enter the peace and rest of His love

The victory is ours He's paid the price
Rise up and walk His faith will suffice
For in these times when troubles arise
Christ shows us in Him all power lies

Always

Always keep your eyes on Jesus
Always let His light shine in
Always let Him lead and guide you
Through life's trials trust in Him

Always keep your eyes on Jesus
Always let his love shine in
For true happiness you'll find
Always resting in Him

God's Hand is Upon You

When circumstances come and
you're in the midst of turmoil
Remember God's hand is upon you

When you've stood for what's right
and by friends feel forsaken
Remember God's hand is upon you

When the day seems heavy with the
clouds of despair
and you fall to your knees
crying out in prayer
pleading for guidance yet sure
He's not hearing
Remember God's hand is upon you

Though the words seem to bounce right
back from the ceiling
and comfort seems far from soul's reach
The direction you're seeking
He'll soon be revealing
Remember God's hand is upon you

God's timing is perfect
He makes no mistakes
Just place yourself into His care
Through these trails He'll take you
He'll mold you and make you
Remember God's hand is upon you

Why

We wonder why things happen the way they do
we look for deep meaning, search for understanding
Why should there be hurt in this world
when there could be happiness
Why do we see the bad in others
instead of looking for the good
Why the loneliness of separation
when we could be together
Why aren't we doing what we really want to do
instead of doing what we don't want to do
We try to appease ourselves
blaming our actions on others
on things that happened or didn't happen
We are told to put the things of our past behind us
to move forward, toward the higher calling
The word of God tells us if we call on him
He will answer and cause our thoughts
to become agreeable to His will
and so our plans will be established
and in Him we will succeed
He never said it would be easy
but he did say it would be possible
It all comes down to choices

He has given us the opportunity to choose
We can choose to follow Him or not
live a life of faith or not
believe His word to be infallible or not
praise Him or complain
make the most of a situation
or allow the situation to overtake us
We have the choice whether we see ourselves
as Jesus sees us
or as the enemy would want us to see ourselves
God's word says we are more than conquerors
Are we truly God's handiwork
or do we see ourselves as a mistake
The choice is ours to make
The word of God tells us
to hunger and thirst after His righteousness
If we spend our time pursuing Jesus
laboring to enter his rest
maybe our choice wouldn't be so hard to make
God wants us to choose
choose Him
choose his way
Maybe that's why
things happen
the way they do

Poems About
Special Occasions of Life

Christmas Observations and Thoughts

Christmas is a magical time of year when people seem to take on a new or different personality. The whole world becomes a happier, more colorful place. The shy step out of the closet and dare to catch an eye, smile or risk saying Merry Christmas to a stranger. Challenging or rude personalities we have to deal with on a regular basis soften and become more bearable. Those carrying a seemingly impenetrable wall around them lower their guard and become just a little more vulnerable. Estranged family members who somehow got lost in life often find their way back home at this special time of year and receive the gift of healing when given the opportunity to make amends. Pockets that appeared to be sewn shut, open and give to causes never given to before.

This time of year hope is often restored as we sense a measure of peace, contentment and joy in the somewhat frustrated world we live in. Maybe there's more to the reason for the season than we can see.

Christmastime

As we celebrate
the birth of Jesus Christ
God's precious gift to mankind
May His love give us
reason to smile
And His joy fill our hearts
with a new passion
To share with others
what Christmas really means

"The Word became flesh and made his dwelling among us."
John 1:14

To Someone Special at Christmas

A friend is someone special
a friend is someone dear
Although many miles apart
a friend is always near

A friend is one who walks right in
and makes themselves at home
And always seems to be there
when you feel alone

A friend is one with whom
you share your joys and fears
A friend is especially thought of
as Christmastime draws near

At this wonderful time of year
this note is sent to read
Merry Christmas and God Bless You
you're a true friend indeed

Easter Observations and Thoughts

Easter is the anniversary of the greatest sacrifice for mankind that has ever been recorded in history. This human sacrifice was given for mankind which in turn gave each and every one of us a second chance in life.

When I reflect on the true meaning of Easter, I often feel it's like a paradox. I feel so small, with so little to offer in light of what was given me. And yet at the same time how valuable am I in the sight of God that He would orchestrate all this for me, for us. At times we appear to be a seemingly thankless species that He created for himself.

And yet…He laid his life down for us…He never gives up on us.

He's Alive

He's alive Praise God He's alive
were the shouts that first Easter Day

But over the years many people
have hardened and gone astray

Now it's time for us God's children
to rise once more and proclaim

He's Alive praise God He's alive
He's alive receive Him today

The Light Arrives

Oh Hallelujah is all I can say
When I think of what Jesus has done for me today

Oh Praise the Lord is what I shout
When in depth I understand what the cross is all about

Oh Glory to God is what I proclaim
When I realize from that day life will never be the same

You are my light Lord
You are my song

You are my strength Lord
All the day long

Marriage

The love of two people
and the love of the Lord
Is like a three stranded cord

It's strength will hold you together
through life's journey
As husband and wife

If invited He will join you
In His wisdom
He'll direct your way

He'll shower His love on you
In the sunshine
Of each happy day you share

And be your strong anchor
When life's storms
Come your way

Marriage is a beautiful union
God Bless you
as you start this journey of love

Texas bluebonnets bravely peek out
from under a cover of snow

A Child's Dedication

Long ago when Jesus walked in Galilee
Children found a welcome at the Savior's knee
All these precious little ones young and old drew near
To hear the wondrous stories in His words so dear

Today we dedicate our precious child to you
Seeking your guidance to teach your word so true
Please help us to be your example in everything we do
And may our child be drawn to sit at your knee too

Poems about
Difficult Times in Life

Get Well Soon

I know you're getting sick of bed
You feel like jumping out
But friend let me tell you
You'd give an awful shout

So just relax and keep it cool
Every day you're getting better
Though doctor's orders never cease
Obey them to the letter

The nurses seem to be right there
To check you on the hour
With lots of needles, lots of pills
And drinks you're sure are sour

Yet all that tender loving care
You're getting there in bed
Will help you to grow stronger
Every day you move ahead

So keep that twinkle in your eye
And grin across your face
Remember keep them happy
As down the halls they race

For the Lord is with you and you've got
A Special job to do
To show the love of Jesus
To all that come to you

Out of the Cage

Sometimes life seems to be in sync
And everything just flows
I feel ok on top of the world
And that's the way it goes

Sometimes it feels I'm in a cage
I don't know what to do
I want to shout and scream out loud
And no one has a clue

Life isn't always fair it seems
I don't always get to choose
The trials are many and some I win
And there are some I lose

I know there is a greater plan
It's just not always clear
So help me Lord to embrace each day
And trust instead of fear

"Praise be to the Lord, to God our Savior,
who daily bears our burdens." Psalm 68:19

The Walk of Love

I saw the look in your eye
Of pain as you walked by

Your heart broken & inside you cry
Listening to yet another lie

Betrayed by one you call a friend
Who hurt & abandoned you in the end

Misunderstood & rejected you feel
A pain so deep how can it heal

Struggling to forgive, for restoration you pray
Asking for mercy & strength for the day

Then you take another breath & you try once more
To walk in love as you did before

"A friend loves at all times…" Proverbs 17:17

The Haven

Sometimes we go through hell
to try to save our souls
But friends I'm here to tell you
that's not the way to go

Some say that it's through
sickness or failure we must go
For that's the only way
for God to make us whole

Some say if friends forsake us
we're rejected and in fear
That that's the only way
to feel that God is near

But God has made a better way
a haven for our soul
He gave His Son named Jesus
now that's the way to go

No fears nor ills nor striving
to sanctify our soul
Can work the work that Jesus can
to cleanse and make us whole

Prayer

Through prayer lives can be put in order
the broken hearted can be healed
Through prayer a lonely day can be made shorter
and a truth within our heart revealed

Through prayer we'll be shown the key to the doors
to set the captive free
Through prayer we can travel to distant shores
with a burden for all God's truth to see

Through prayer we can see blind eyes opened
and the sick in body healed
Through prayer God's word has been spoken
and His perfect love revealed

Through prayer we can pull someone out of the mire
and rejoice as their life begins to turn
Yes prayer is the spark to many a fire
as revival begins to burn

Prayer takes time and it takes persistence
Yet it can change the course of our existence

Poems of Faith
and Commitment

Your Mercy

Your mercy flows like a river
Washing over the soul

Bringing peace and forgiveness
To a sinner once more

God you are steadfast
You never give up

You keep showering your children
With unfailing love

And just when I think
I have nowhere to go

You come in like a flood
And wash me once more

Oh God of mercy God of love
Thank you for your unending love

Healed

He said believe and you shall be healed
I cried Lord help me to believe

He said pray and it shall be done
Teach me I asked as I laid down before him

He said child of God you must walk in faith
I asked him to fill me and I declared his word

He said give and it shall be given unto thee
I gave him my life to serve him each day

He said wait and the power will come from on high
And I waited and saw the hand of God

Take Me

Lord take me to the nations
Where the fields are ripe
And many need to know
Lord I cry take me I'll go

Lord your word says ask
And you will receive
Lord today I ask for
The souls of many
Lord take me to the nations
I'll go

"Many are the plans in a person's heart,
but it is the LORD's purpose that prevails."
Proverbs 19:21

Show Me

Lord I put my hope in you
I trust in you and I pray
That you will guide my steps
and show me the right way

For life is full of options
The choices I must make
Some roads are very easy
And others so hard to take

I know that you will guide me
You promise that you will
And yet I find it difficult
Even though my heart you fill

The sting of isolation
The love of one so dear
You know my every desire
There is no need to fear

You are the strength that rises
From deep within my heart
The plan you have is perfect
Please show me where to start

Your Unfailing Love

Lord help me put into words
What you have done for me
To express your unfailing love
So others you may see

Lord reveal your bountiful grace
Extend unmerited favor
To those who are lost
And in need of you as a Savior

You paid for my atonement
A life sacrifice you gave
Reconciling me with God
That from sin I could be saved

You washed me white as snow
And sanctified my soul
You filled me with your love
Then freed me to become whole

You sent your Holy Spirit
To guide me on life's way
He freely gave me gifts
To empower me each day

By faith I was justified
As in my heart I believed
Lord may others also find
This joy and peace I received

You gave me all I need
Through your mercy love and grace
Help me be an expression
Of you to the human race

Poems about
Life and Death

His Coming

Miracle of miracles
When Jesus Christ we see
Coming through the clouds
His children to receive

With the sound of the trumpet
In the twinkling of an eye
To the arms of our dear Savior
We will meet Him in the sky

Soaring through the clouds
Towards the heavenly throne
The world and its cares behind us
Approaching our new home

Miracle of miracles
When Jesus Christ we see
All those who are waiting for Him
Shall with Him forever be

The Transition

Death is but a transition
when a life changes position
When freedom comes from all
pain and tears
With time no longer measured
by hours or by years

Death is but the changing
from here to heaven above
When the ones you held so dear
rest in our Father's love

Hebrews 9:16 (The Message Bible)
"Like a will that takes effect when someone dies,
the new covenant was put into action at Jesus' death.
His death marked the transition from the old plan
to the new one, canceling the old obligations
and accompanying sins and summoning the heirs
to receive the eternal inheritance
that was promised them. He brought together
God and His people in this new way."

Reflections

Blessed be the Lord God Almighty
He makes no mistakes
His ways are just
His timing ever perfect
He gives life and takes life away

Who is man that we should question
or dispute the mind of God
His ways are perfect
He knows our every thought, our hopes,
our fears, our successes and our failures
And knowing the sinful heart of man
He still loves us

He loves us, you and me, so much
that He sent His only Son Jesus to die
Death was the price He had Jesus pay for our sins
so that we may have an opportunity to live

Yet we have a choice, life or death
Life fuller and richer here and
life everlasting for eternity
Or death, while we strive to live for ourselves and
are doomed for an eternity of separation
I pray that today you would choose life
Choose Jesus, our only hope for eternity

My dad suffered with Alzheimer's. I wrote this poem when he passed away and read it as a tribute to his life at his funeral. I am so thankful that years earlier, while he was able, he committed his life to Jesus. He had his shortcomings like each of us do, yet he had hope in the saving grace of Jesus Christ. Because of that hope I have full confidence that he is in heaven, and for this reason we could rejoice when he was able to leave this earth to be with the Lord. My prayer is that each and every one will choose Jesus while there is still time to do so.

Her Last Breath

She watched for death as if watching for a friend
Then drew her last breath and that was the end
As with grace she slipped into eternity

Hand in hand with Jesus she was heaven bound
Her vibrant new body walking tall and strong
You could almost hear her laugh as they went along

She danced she sang she shouted with glee
Greeting all who had passed whom now she could see
Enveloped in peace she was finally home

Then she stopped for a moment and glanced my way
As if to tell me that all was well, she was ok
Then she nodded, turned and was gone

Her life she gave to God years before
Recognized Him as her Savior knew He was the door
To eternity His presence and love for evermore

Her prayer for her family each day while on earth
Was that all would experience this second birth
Give their hearts to Christ and live for Him

So her message I am here to share
Don't wait any longer place yourself in God's care
So that one day you too can join her up there

I wrote this poem about my mom and read it at her funeral. At the age of 90 she was diagnosed with cancer and spent eight months in the hospital waiting to go to heaven. I had the privilege of sitting with her for many of those months, an opportunity for which I will forever be grateful. Most of our conversations were about heaven, what dying would be like and her wondering when she would finally be able to go. She could hardly wait to meet her Lord face to face. As per her wishes I had the blessing of holding her hand while she peacefully slipped into eternity.

In the Arms of God

In the arms of God
The safest place to be
When life's storms rage
It's His face I see

When I cry in pain
He wipes away my tears
When doubt comes my way
He keeps me from all fears

No need to question
He's always just
His love suffices
In Him I trust

My hope for tomorrow
His name is healing
Resting in His arms
What a joyous feeling

"His faithful promises are your
armor and protection." Psalm 91:4

Poems about
Special People in Life

There are many different people who walk through our lives, some for a very short time and some for a lifetime. Each one plays a part of who we become. Some are a vital part, like family, whom we can't imagine living without. Some show up for a season, to share an intense moment or experience and then they're gone. Some impact our lives so heavily that they will never be forgotten, touching our lives in a profound way. Writing about all the different people who make us who we are would take a book in itself.

Mom

When God created you he had a plan
and a purpose for your life
He gave you an important job
as a godly mother and a wife

Life sometimes made you laugh
and at times you wanted to scream
With all of its ups and downs
sometimes it felt more like a dream

Many nights you woke with a nudge
and the Lord would have you pray
For God's protection for your children
that they seek Him and not lose their way

At times now you feel forgotten
and you wonder why you're still here
Remember your work will be over
in God's timing; it's perfect and clear

You'll receive a healthy new body
when the Lord comes to take you home
You'll join those who have gone before you
singing praises at God's throne

"Truly I am your servant, Lord;
I serve you just as my mother did;
you have freed me from my chains."   Psalm 116:15-17

I wrote this poem and read it at my mom's "Almost 90" birthday party. Her health had been declining so we, her children, decided not to wait for her birth date, but rather to give her a party while she could still enjoy it, to honor her and show her how much she meant to us. It turned out to be everything we hoped it would be for her. She was beaming the whole weekend and spent the rest of her life showing people her party pictures. We were so thankful we could do this for her. She was hospitalized a month before her actual birthday and remained there until her death.

The Bond of Friendship

Sometimes I feel there's a chasm between us
So big it gives me a chill
No words are spoken but I can feel it
Why does it make me feel ill
When did this happen and what went wrong
With regrets tears my eyes fill

Conversations are now superficial and hollow
Is this how you want it to be
I struggle to hold on as you push me away
Why is it that you can't see
I'm a person not an object that you discard
To value one another is a key

Friendship is a bond not merely an acquaintance
It's a necessity for living
A treasure of mutual affection and value
That only works in giving
It will only thrive and can't survive
Unless we keep forgiving

Through friendship one helps the other grow
God had this all in mind
An important part of this world to me
You're definitely one of a kind
So please don't give up or toss us aside
As true friendship is hard to find

"…But there is a friend that sticketh closer
than a brother." Proverbs 18:24

My Love

My love I don't know what to say
When things fall around you day by day

With all the troubles in the world
And the need for things one can't afford

I fear you're getting far too uptight
And oft times think you have the right

But we must remember what the Lord said
And give our cares to Him instead

Oh I know it isn't easy to do
But the Lord above is faithful and true

And I believe if He sees that we do try
He'll also give us patience by and by

Graduation Day

It seems like only yesterday
Our little girl was born
And now you've finished high school
With feelings slightly torn

Excitement and anticipation
Of the future that lies ahead
Mixed with emotions when realizing
The good-byes that need to be said

Though the path the Lord has for you
May not always seem so clear
In His wisdom He will guide you
As you trust instead of fear

We pray God's peace upon you
Wherever you may go
May the love and joy of Jesus
Be what you to others show

I wrote this poem for our eldest daughter, Tara, when she graduated from high school. She was our first child and we were so proud of her, and yet had mixed emotions as she closed this chapter of her life and moved into a new era, so to speak, with more independence and adventures.

Son

Son you are a special gift
  Given from above
From the day that you were born
  You filled our hearts with love

As a child you played for hours
  Life seemed to pass you by
Contentment was your nature
  Seldom did you cry

Then as you grew you often felt
  You didn't really fit
So you set out to find yourself
  No longer would you sit

Along the way you met your mate
  Someone to understand
Who seemed to fill the gap you felt
  And lend a helping hand

In diligence and faithfulness
  You've worked hard all these years
With kindness God has gifted you
  Pride fills our eyes with tears

The Wait

We've waited a long time for a child to come along
To complete our family as together we'll belong
Our hearts skip a beat and we try to stay on our seat
As our social worker tells of our first big meet

Could it be true? It's hard to believe
That soon our awaited we will receive
Our heads are spinning as she tells us what seems
All the details that fill all our hopes and our dreams

Oh Lord we pray… may all go well
As we visit our child and prepare to dwell
In one home as one family each with the other
Two girls, one boy, a father and mother

We're so happy that she'll be our little girl
More precious than gold or a costly pearl
Through life's ups and downs we'll together grow
As a family with God's love the way to show

A Tribute to a Friend

Sometimes you're my Chiro Neuro
Sometimes you are my hero
At times you're more like a brother
But definitely from another mother
And yet you're also my friend
On whom I can depend

Sometimes you make me glad
Sometimes you hurt me and I'm sad
At times when I'm ready to quit
And I feel like throwing a fit
You make me laugh and we forget
The reasons why we were upset

You make it easy to share from the heart
And if needed give me a new start
Life hasn't always been an easy flow
Yet you never quit as on you go
You've worked hard, got to laugh and sing
And experience small miracles that only God can bring

I thank God he gave me you as a friend
May your passion to help others never end
May your gifting to teach expand
And help more people than ever planned
You're one of a kind this I hope you can see
Thank you for who you are to me

One day I had an accident that changed my life. I suddenly joined the ranks of the disabled. Seemingly endless trips to doctors, physical therapy, MRIs, x-rays, surgeries, treatments and never-ending bumps in the road became my life. To retrain my body, I had to learn to do things I used to without thinking.

This poem is for one of the great doctors whom I believe the Lord brought into my life. He has given me countless hours of help with the challenges that have come my way. Over the years our relationship has taken on many faces. Although I know the Lord put this man in my life to help bring healing to me, I also believe God has a special plan through this for him. I pray a hundredfold blessing for him.

"Give and it shall be given unto thee,
pressed down and running over..." Luke 6:38

Poems of Hope
and Forgiveness

The Robe

One day I had a vision while traveling down the road
I saw myself before the King dressed in a robe
This robe was very different than any seen before
It hung to my feet all filthy and torn like a
Ragged garment no repair could make it whole
I felt so hopeless and sadness gripped my soul

Then I realized this scene depicted me how
Sin had torn my life beyond repair it seemed
There was no human way to fix what sin had wrought
Desperately I cried out to God His mercy I sought
Confessing all my sins He was faithful and true
Cleansing my unrighteousness He filled me anew

The scene then changed the hand of Christ I saw
He removed the dirty robe that
Disappeared as it fell to the ground
At once I saw a new robe so white and pure and clean
God's love beyond compare new hope it brought me

"This robe," He said, "is my mercy and my grace
To cover your sin and restore your life of faith"
I felt a new strength in me and looking up I saw
My King and Lord smile on this child of God
No words can express the peace that came to me
As forgiveness flowed from Him on the throne
When I brought my all to God

"Now Joshua was clothed with filthy garments, and
stood before the angel. And he answered and spake
unto those that stood before him, saying, Take away
the filthy garments from him. And unto him he said,
Behold, I have caused thine iniquity to pass from thee,
and I will clothe thee with change of raiment."
Zachariah 3:3-4

"If we confess our sins,
he is faithful and just to forgive us our sins,
and to cleanse us from all unrighteousness." 1 John 1:9

Forgiven

Oh to receive forgiveness
The blessed relief from sin
One cannot live without it
And yet find peace within

Oh to receive this freedom
That only Christ can give
When we cry out for forgiveness
New life we start to live

Oh to receive the joy
That Jesus alone can bring
As we relinquish all our burdens
A new song our heart will sing

He is God

Fear thou not; For I am with thee
Were His words when aloneness came
Then growing from down deep within came
a peace that leaves one never the same
Jesus is Peace and only He can be
The changing of all fears to free

Be not dismayed; for I am thy God
When I looked around and all I saw
seemed to be to me such utter confusion
In this world and His children
there seemed such disillusion
Then my eyes returned to focus on Him
And then I saw the hand of God

I will strengthen thee; yea I will help thee
Was His promise when circumstances grew
And overwhelmed by the mountains
all at once I knew
Only He has the strength to carry me through

I will uphold thee with the right hand
of my righteousness
He reminded when I seemed unsure
How he'd chosen me before the making
of the world
How His love holds me secure

Your sins are all covered in
My Blood
He spoke as He gently poured
forth His Love
Now go and give to all you see
with hunger in their heart
My love I send and peace impart
To give each life a brand new start

"Fear thou not, for I am with thee;
be not dismayed, for I am thy God;
I will strengthen thee; yea, I will
help thee; yea, I will uphold
thee with the right hand of
my righteousness..." Isaiah 41:10

Author Karen Klassen

I have taken my own life experiences, as well as those of others around me, and put them into poetry to encourage, bring hope, and at times challenge the reader to see life from another plane or dimension. I met and married the love of my life as a teenager and am the mother of 3 children and have 7 grandchildren.

I enjoyed a career in nursing, specializing in labor and delivery, giving me the privilege of caring for others and sharing in the miracle of birth.

My husband and I have served as missionaries for close to 30 years and are the founders of Harvest Field Ministries. The focus of the ministry is to bring the hope of Jesus Christ to the poor and equip or empower the nationals in their countries.

In my life I have been challenged with many different health issues, which were instrumental in growing my faith. God has granted me miraculous healings and used the hands of medical doctors to bring restoration to my body.

I have personally seen God's hand of provision in my life and in the lives of those I've been privileged to be part of.

In life you sometimes have to go through
doors of unknown challenges to see
the beauty on the other side

CPSIA information can be obtained at www.ICGtesting.com
Printed in the USA
LVIW01n0703030216
473439LV00001B/1